AF218970

How to buy and fly a quadcopter droꞁᷤ
Roland Büchi

Bibliografische Information der Deutschen Nationalbibliothek
Die Deutsche Nationalbibliothek verzeichnet diese Publikation in
der Deutschen Nationalbibliografie; detaillierte bibliografische
Daten sind im Internet über www.dnb.de abrufbar.

Impressum
© Roland Büchi, 2022, 2nd edition
Herstellung und Verlag: BoD – Books on Demand,
Norderstedt
ISBN: 978-3-7557-7844-8

Contents

1. Ready-to-fly quadcopters

Figure 1: RTF- quadcopter.

At the beginning of the development of quadcopters in the early 2000s one had to buy all the components separately. At that time there were only a few complete systems. So you had to assemble the systems by yourself – control electronics, brushless controllers, motors, propellers and frame. Then you had to download the appropriate software for the system. In those days, this kind of construction required a good level of technical knowledge about the function of each component.

But the ongoing development of the electronics in recent years means that quadcopters are today mainly purchased by users as complete systems and RTF ('ready to fly'). So today, for the pure fun of flying it is no longer absolutely necessary to understand the technology of these fascinating systems to the finest detail. And that's good because in this way quadcopter systems can be made accessible to many model pilots.

Often there are model pilots from other sectors, e.g. aircraft, helicopter, car or ship model builders, who simply buy and fly such aircraft out of curiosity. Or there are complete newbies who have never previously come into contact with flight models.

The 'ready to fly' market goes hand in hand with a substantial price reduction. In the early years of development it was still necessary to pay about the same price for a quadcopter as for a large model helicopter, making many people think twice about whether they really want to start this hobby. Today, however, one sees quadcopters in all sizes and price ranges on the market. They start with the toy quadcopters, which are small and, despite their low price, often surprisingly robust, and finish with big quadcopters with several kilograms of weight and a payload to transport cameras for photo flight.

In this model division, a similar trend can be observed as with helicopter and airplane models. The smaller and cheaper systems are often built as 'ready to fly', while larger systems are often available as kits, with the possibility of software downloading and the installation of extensions, e.g. photo flight or GPS systems.

1.1   Indoors - outdoors

Figures 1 and 2 show RTF quadcopters which you can buy for a relatively small amount of money and which promise good fun flight already after a few minutes. You just need to take the quadcopter out of the box and charge the battery, and you're ready. The size comparison with a credit card shows that even quite small miniature quadcopters can be built. The question of whether such systems can be operated both indoors and outdoors then arises. The situation is similar with model helicopters. In both cases, the smaller systems are more suitable for indoors, because of their small size. They often have too small a thrust to be used outdoors. This causes problems with the wind influences. They will sometimes be completely blown away. As soon as the systems are slightly larger than the smallest format, you can go outside on windless days and risk some test flights. From a propeller size of about 4 inches (about 10 cm) the produced thrust is quite suitable for use outdoors and the quadcopter is also able to withstand light wind influence. Then it is also really interesting for outdoor flights undertaken with built-in cameras.

Figure 2: RTF quadcopters can be quite small – here compared to a credit-card-sized card.

1.2   Package

Such RTF models can include different features. Mostly, however, it is so that in addition to the completely assembled quadcopter, the radio control and maybe even a small battery charger are also included. Often in very small systems, the battery of the radio control is tapped as a charger to recharge the battery. Many quadcopters can also be charged via a USB cable directly from a PC.

But the packages of RTF models today in many cases also include other accessories. Figure 3 shows a quadcopter with camera and other sensors during flight. It is one of those systems which in the basic equipment can be purchased as RTF along with the radio control. But here a lot more is included than with small systems. For example, even a GPS is built in. Thus the quadcopter can hold its current position when you press a button on the radio control, or it can avoid collisions with sensors. In addition, this quadcopter has also a built- in camera. Thus it is ready for photo and film flights. There is even the possibility to put a smartphone on the radio control and watch what is being filmed. Of course, such complete systems are more expensive than those which were shown above. When purchasing one, you should always first consider what extension components you would like to use later and find out whether they are also available for these systems.

Figure 3: Quadcopter in action.

1.3 Integrated camera

A good example of an RTF quadcopter system with integrated video system is illustrated in Figures 4 and 5. A camera is already installed in this quadcopter. The radio control even includes a display. This shows the transmitted images from the camera already during the flight. So the model pilot can see the transmitted image data while also keeping visual contact with the quadcopter. He may just feel as if he were sitting directly in the cockpit himself. This is a so- called online data transmission. Here, the images and films are transferred during the flight. There are also systems with offline data transmission available. Here, during the flight there is no opportunity to access the photos and movies.

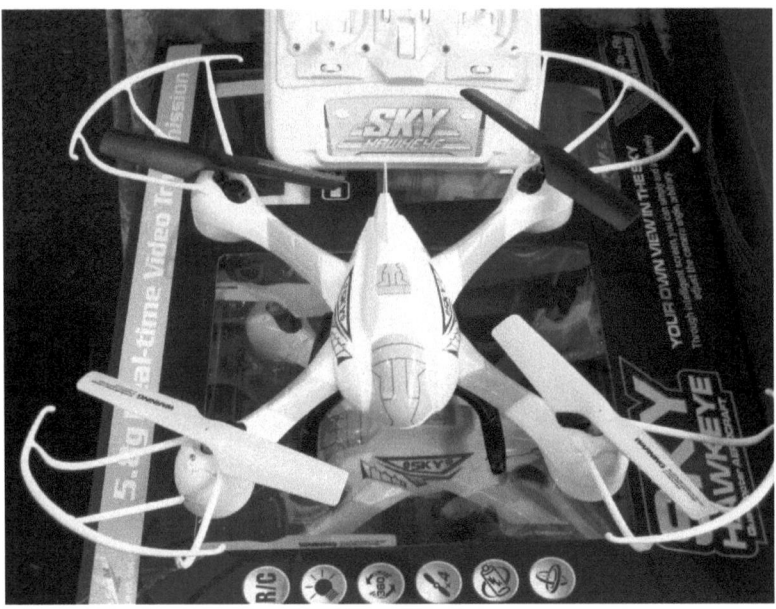

Figure 4: Quadcopter with integrated camera.

In many quadcopters additional functions are included which can produce great effects in the air. There are some which can fly autonomous figures at your fingertips on the radio control. This may for example be a flip, so a fast rotation around the pitch or roll axis or a rotation around the vertical axis, or the trajectory of a figure of eight.

The trend is clearly that in the future there will be even more RTF quadcopters on the market. Extension functions are then already available in the basic version or can easily be plugged in. A lot of features such as cameras or GPS will increasingly be offered already out of the box or as a complete set. In the future, the user will be confronted even less with the software and configuration. He will be able to activate the components just by switching a lever on the radio control. And many systems will detect by themselves which component is currently active.

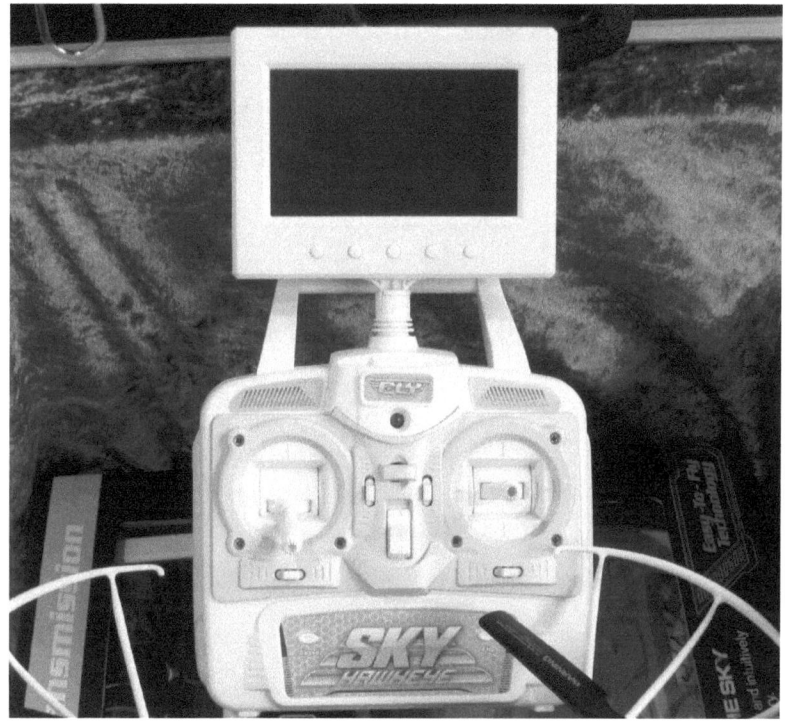

Figure 5: Radio control with integrated display.

2   Functionality

Quadcopters are aircraft with four propellers. They have the same control capabilities as helicopters. Figure 6 illustrates this. The stick assignment of the radio control, as shown in Figure 7, is most commonly selected. However there are also model pilots who swap the left and right sides.

Figure 6: Control capabilities.

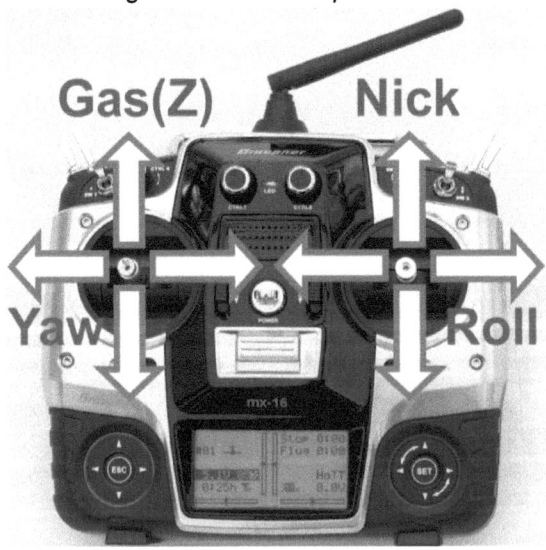

Figure 7: Stick assignment.

'Nick' describes the tilting forward and backward. For that purpose, the stick of the remote control needs to be moved upwards (tilting forward) and downwards (tilting backward).

'Roll' describes the tilting to the left and right. The stick needs to be moved to the left and the right side.

'Yaw' describes the rotation around the vertical axis (z). The left stick needs to be moved to the left (counterclockwise yaw, view from top side) or the right (clockwise yaw, view from top side).

'Gas' describes the movement along the vertical axis (z). If the left stick is moved down, it means descent flight, and if the left stick is moved up into the full throttle position, it means climb flight.

2.1   Movement

The immediate question is now how a quadcopter can be controlled physically with the above functions.

A helicopter will again serve as a comparison. Anyone who has ever built and flown helicopters knows that this requires quite a complex mechanism. A hard landing is rarely forgiven: bent rods, ragged ball heads and expensive repairs are the consequence. Many have thus abandoned the model helicopter hobby, the so-called pinnacle of model aircraft. 'Nick' and 'Roll' is realized with a so-called swash plate. This provides at the end an angle-shift of the main rotor force axis to the fuselage. 'Gas' is provided by 'pitching', which is achieved by changing the pitch of the rotor blades. 'Yaw' is realized by a change in speed of the tail rotor. Some models also reach yaw by pitching the tail rotor blades.

Quadcopters, which – as mentioned above – have the same control options as helicopters, in contrast stand out by virtue of their much simpler and thereby massively less sensitive mechanics: There are four motors, which are rigidly connected with two right- and two left-rotating propellers – and that's all. Everything else is provided by a little electronic control board. Figure 8 illustrates this.

'Nick' is physically achieved by a change in speed of the upper and lower propeller (see Figure 8). To move the quadcopter in the X direction, the lower propeller is turning faster and the upper one slower. Thus, an inclination in the direction of the x-axis is achieved.

'Roll' is achieved by a change in speed of the left and right propeller. A movement in the Y direction requires a higher speed of the right and a lower speed of the left propeller.

The main rotor of a helicopter produces a torque about the vertical axis (z) because of its twisting. The tail rotor serves to compensate for that torque. The two right- and left-rotating propellers of the quadcopter do this job instead. Thus a tail rotor is not needed. 'Yaw' is achieved by ensuring that both left and right propellers have a different speed than both upper and lower ones. A counter-clockwise yaw (viewed from above) requires a higher speed of the upper and lower propeller and a lower speed of the left and right one.

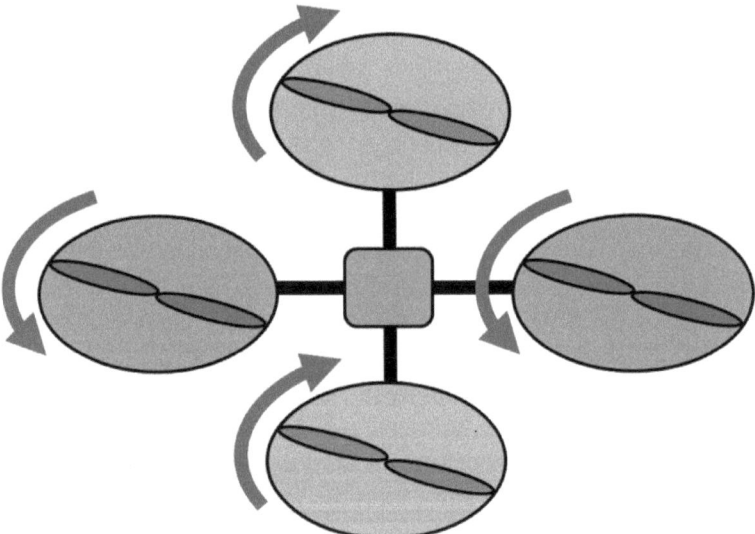

Figure 8: Two left- and right-rotating propellers, view from top side.

A change in 'Gas' requires a change in the speed of all propellers together. During the climb flight, all propellers have a higher speed. As mentioned above, Quadcopters and helicopters are controlled by the same functions and also have the same possibilities of movement – almost. Because of the control over the speed of the propellers it is not possible to fly stably overhead and to 'mow the lawn', as some pilots demonstrate with their pitch-controlled helicopters. However, loops are possible with Quadcopters. They are flown as with a model airplane, where the gas is taken away close to the apex and strongly accelerated for the subsequent stabilization in the suspense position.

2.2   Flight configurations, '+' and 'x' and others

Quadcopters can be configured in the '+' and 'x' orientation. This is shown in Figure 9. Here, the arrow is pointing in the forward direction. It is apparent that the booms of the quadcopter represent a '+' or an 'x'. Most of the today's quadcopters are configured in the 'x' configuration, to allow a better camera mounting in the front. With an even larger number of rotating propellers with hexacopters or octocopters you can imagine many different possibilities in which these can be arranged.

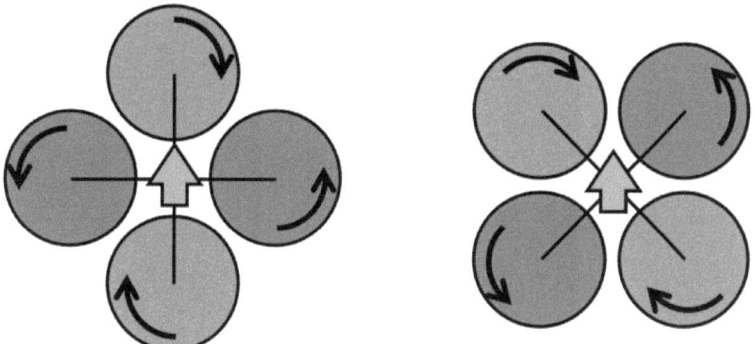

Figure 9: '+' and 'x' propeller arrangement of quadcopters.

Figure 10 shows a possible arrangement of the propellers of a hexacopter. These are arranged annularly and each boom is connected to the center. The control electronics is usually mounted here. It would also be possible that the motors are mounted on an outer ring. Then three or four booms would connect it to the center. There is now a difference whether the arrow, which means the front, points in the direction of a boom or whether it points in the direction between two booms. Here it is already somewhat difficult to call this a '+' or 'x' arrangement. The booms describe neither of these. One might denote the left figure as 'I' arrangement and the right as a 'V' arrangement. But these terms are not even necessary and one can simply let the figures speak. For the torque compensation of the yaw axis, three left-rotating and three right-rotating propellers have to be mounted. These are then placed alternately in the direction of rotation.

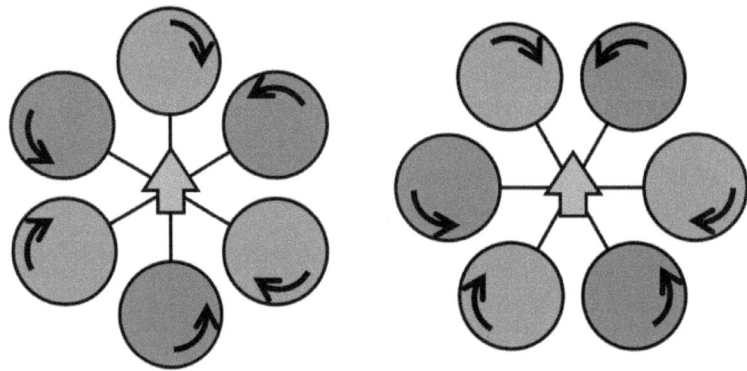

Figure 10: Annular propeller assembly of hexacopters.

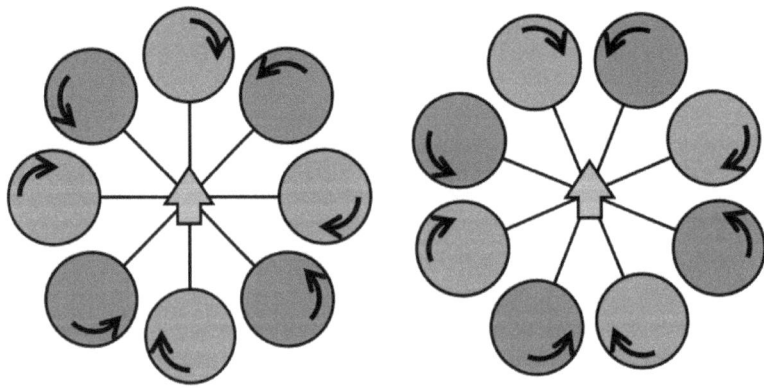

Figure 11: Annular propeller assembly of octocopters.

14

Figure 11 shows the same with annularly arranged propellers of octocopters. Here, too, the arrow points in the one figure in the direction of a boom and in the other between two booms. Since 2 x 4 = 8, one octocopter is actually also two quadcopters. Arrangements like that shown in Figure 12 are therefore also built, although somewhat less frequently.

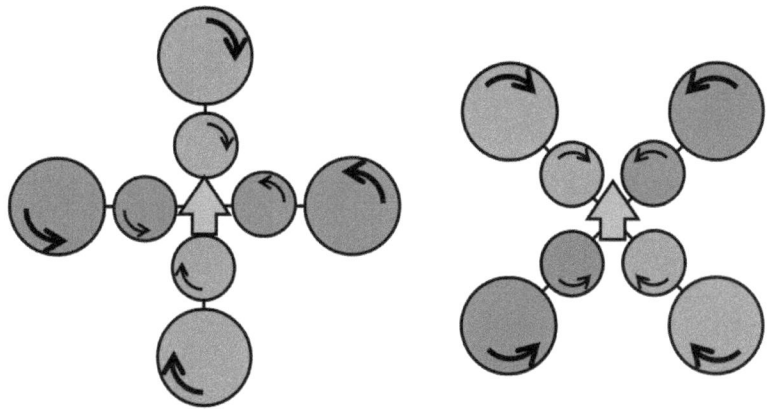

Figure 12: Other options for the propeller arrangement in octocopters.

Here two motors and propellers sit on a boom. In this way it is possible to save some weight at the frame structure. In addition, the '+' and 'x' arrangement can be nicely seen here again. For geometric reasons the inner motors and propellers can also be made somewhat smaller than the outer ones. The control is the same as with quadcopters. The two drives on the same axis will both receive the same control signal. However, a closer look at this system shows that the overall size of the system isn't optimal in the propeller area. The inner propellers already take some space away and between the outer ones there are larger empty spaces.

Hexacopters and octocopters are sometimes also built in the so-called H-arrangement according to Figure 13. In this case, all the motors and propellers are located on two sides lengthwise. With a little imagination you can recognize here the letter H. Again, the motors and propellers are typically mounted alternately left- and right-turning.

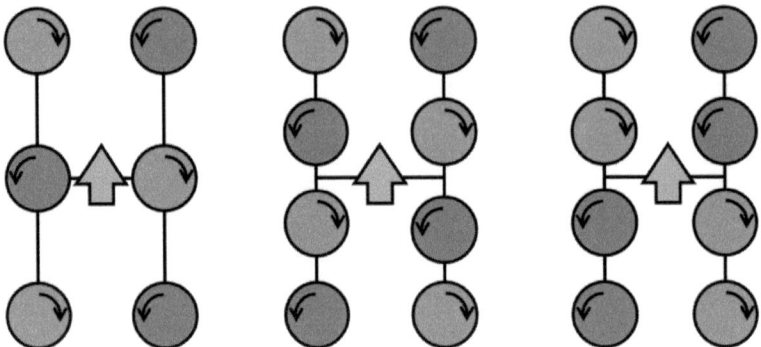

Figure 13: H-arrangement of hexacopters and octocopters.

Figure 14: Quadcopter in 'x'- configuration.

2.3 How to buy

At this point, some decision support on the purchase is given. This is a very brief summary.

'+' or 'x' orientation	Mostly 'x', to allow a better camera mounting in the front
	Outdoors: highly visible fuselage recommended
Propeller size	Indoors: about from 2" to 6"
	Outdoors: beginners: about 4" to 8", experts: 8" and more
Propeller protection	Highly recommended, i.e. EPP material, plastic or carbon rings for safety reasons
Motors	Beginners: brushless DC motors or brushed DC motors
	Experts: brushless DC motors
Frame	Carbon, plastic, EPP
Weight	Beginners: up to 250g flight weight
	Experts: even more than 250g flight weight
	check maximum weight with current legislation
Radio control	Indoors: 2.4 GHz or infrared
	Outdoors: 2.4 GHz
Battery	LiPo, LiFePo, for a flight of 10–15 min. is needed:
	about 12g flight weight: 1S/100mAh
	about 50g flight weight: 1S/450mAh
	about 100g flight weight: 1S/900mAh, 2S/450mAh
	about 200g flight weight: 2S/900mAh, 3S/600mAh
	about 400g flight weight: 3S/1200mAh, 2S/1800mAh
	about 800g flight weight: 4S/1800mAh, 3S/2400mAh
	about 1200g flight weight: 4S/2700mAh, 3S/3600mAh
GPS	Indoors: not needed
	Outdoors: as desired, especially interesting in combination with a camera
Camera	Beginners (low price):
	■ low-price built-in camera with plastic lens
	■ offline data transmission

	Beginners and experts:
	<ul><li>as desired, up to a maximum weight</li><li>offline or online data transmission</li></ul>
Gimbal for camera	Beginners (low price): no gimbal
	Beginners and experts: rotating gimbal

Straight away the question arises of what kind of system you should first practice on. You can fly the flight maneuvers in the following chapters with almost all multicopters. Good advice is not to buy a very expensive system straight away, but a reasonably inexpensive 'ready-to-fly' quadcopter of medium size. A reasonable size would be a propeller size of about 5 inches or 12 cm. Such a quadcopter produces enough thrust to withstand light wind influences outdoors. In addition, propeller protection is important, at least when practicing and even more so later. This often consists of rings of plastic or EPP material. This protects on the one hand oneself and other present people against an uncontrollably crashing quadcopter, but also completely different things such as flowers and the like. On the other hand it also protects the propellers themselves. They are less in danger of kinking or even breaking. There are quite different propellers available for today's quadcopters. There are ones made of glass fiber reinforced plastic (GRP) or carbon or even those made of hard or soft plastic. Specifically, the propellers made of GRP are often very hard and resistant. They have on the one hand the advantage that they can't be destroyed immediately by a hard landing. On the other hand, they have the disadvantage that they can cause damage or even injury. Propellers made of hard plastic or carbon can break relatively quickly on contact with the ground. This can also cause damage or injury. He who has the choice should choose soft plastic propellers, if possible, although they are often not as efficient as other propellers. But they cause less damage or injury than the others. Many RTF quadcopters are equipped with such soft propellers.

3. How to prepare a flight

Flying a quadcopter is something that can be easily learned. However, the idea that this is possible in a single day remains an illusion. As with learning to drive a car you need to follow many steps and practice again and again. This booklet is a mini flight school. The individual steps will be discussed and applied in their own chapters. They are designed so that their difficulty is in ascending order. Most of the flight maneuvers are based on each other. The skipping of chapters may work while reading. When practicing you should, however, only proceed to the next chapter if you have repeatedly practiced the current chapter and can undertake all the corresponding maneuvers reliably. Only in this way can you ensure that you can also learn the more difficult flight maneuvers.

3.1 Simulation software

To practice, various simulation programs are now offered on the market. Some of them also include a radio control. These can be connected via a USB interface to the PC. But there are also radio controls which can be used for operation with real quadcopters and which also run together with a simulation program on the PC via an interface. This is particularly interesting, since then with this radio control one can control a quadcopter either in reality or virtually on-screen. In addition, you can also use other settings such as trims simultaneously in reality and in the simulation.

These programs offer simulation models for many different model airplanes. Also quite different quadcopters can be selected here. Multicopters with four to eight propellers may be included. The exercise with the simulation program certainly makes sense at the beginning. You can perhaps prevent crashing a real quadcopter. In practice, however, it is also a question of your interest in simulation programs, whether and for how long you want to practice on a PC with a virtual aircraft. Ultimately, many quadcopter or model plane pilots choose this hobby precisely to get away from the computers they use for their work. In any case, the exercises which are proposed in the next chapters can be done both in the simulation as well as with real quadcopters. Of course, sooner or later everyone will detach from the simulation and proceed to flying in the real world.

3.2   Insurance

As soon as you want to fly with your real quadcopter, you have to ask yourself the question of insurance. Hopefully, you may never have an accident. If nevertheless something does suddenly happen and it causes damage, you should be prepared. Your insurance provider can advise you on this. They often provide additional services for model airplanes or quadcopters. The relevant conditions vary from country to country and you should do the necessary research into them.

3.3   Starting for practicing

Model helicopters are related to quadcopters concerning their control. Thus, the following quadcopter flight lessons will contain similar elements. For practice with helicopters a training frame is often used. It consists of two crosswise arranged carbon rods with ping pong balls at their ends. This is then mounted for example under the skids. This is done to get a little more stability on the ground and the helicopter doesn't overturn immediately with every not completely soft landing, and so the rotor blades remain intact. For most quadcopters such a training frame is not necessary, since the four booms also more or less form a large cross. The risk of overturning in the event of a somewhat hard landing is therefore already smaller than with helicopters. Those quadcopters which have landing gear on the bottom for the mounting of a camera are therefore not as well suited for practice. They can fall onto the propeller blades in the event of a hard landing. On such quadcopters the landing gear should be removed if possible. A camera is not needed when practicing anyway. In any case, you should be able to tilt the quadcopter in any direction without any of the propellers touching the ground.

When you want to perform the first outdoor flight, you should do it on an almost windless day, if possible. It would be ideal, of course, if you could hire an entire sports hall for yourself, but probably almost no one has this possibility. As starting position you can then place the quadcopter so that the front marked boom is oriented as shown in Figure 15. In this orientation, all booms for nick and roll move in the same direction as you move the sticks of the radio control.

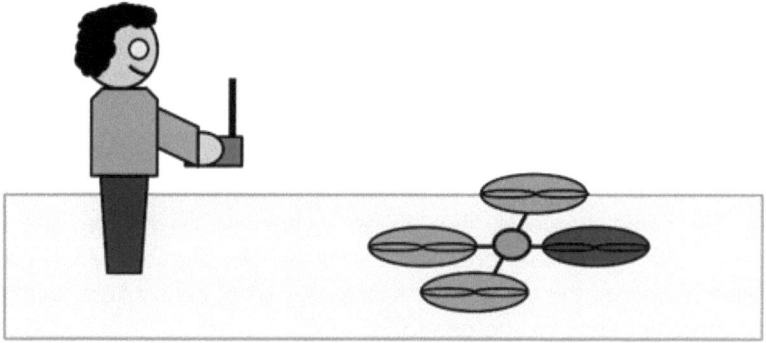

Figure 15: Orientation of the quadcopter before starting, using '+' configuration.

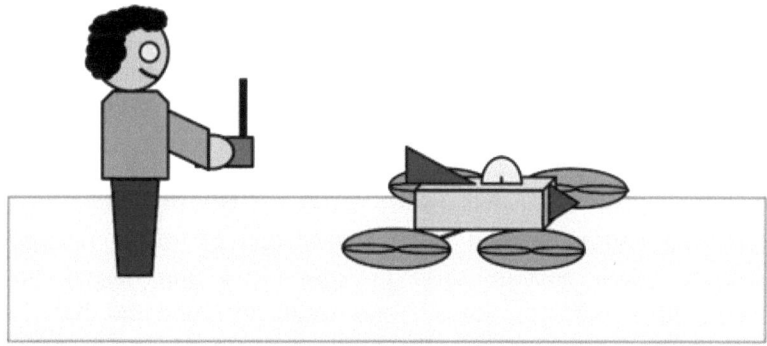

Figure 16: Orientation of the quadcopter before starting, using 'x' configuration.

In most RTF quadcopters the configuration can't be freely selected. Some of these have small fuselage constructions and they can only be flown in 'x' configuration. With these systems, you don't find the orientation with the booms, but according to the fuselage structures. Perhaps the two front booms or even the propellers are marked in a different color. Figure 16 shows how to place this quadcopter before starting. Again, the quadcopter moves in the nick and roll axis the same as you move the sticks in the radio control.

3.4　How to hold the radio control and operate the sticks

Most the currently used transmitters are so-called handheld transmitters. This applies to almost all 'ready-to-fly' quadcopters. As the name suggests, the station is held on each side with a hand. Often the pilots only steer with the two thumbs, which are each placed on the tops of the sticks. For small transmitters, this is the most common way to control.

For larger transmitters, another type of control is to take the stick between your thumb and forefinger. The transmitter will then be clamped with the palms. The author prefers this control type, as in his opinion it allows a more sensitive control. A strap allows for additional fixing. This is worn around the neck. It has the advantage that the transmitter can't slip out of your hands and fall to the ground. However, it is a disadvantage that you need to release the strap first if you want to put the radio control down.

So-called console transmitters are somewhat less frequently used. They are usually shaped so that they can be rested on your stomach. Here another strap provides extra grip. Mostly you control here with your thumb and forefinger, and the hand is supported on the controller. The transmitter will remain in position without the help of the hands. For many larger handheld transmitters extensions to console transmitters are available.

3.5   Function check

Before every flight, you should perform a short function check. This includes testing whether the motors are still firmly bolted to the frame. At the same time you should also check whether the propellers are still fixed on the motor shafts. For example, screws can become loose due to vibrations of the rotating parts. Tighten them if required. If a motor or a propeller were to detach in flight, a crash of the aircraft would immediately result. In addition, without screws, the motors would only be connected to the quadcopter by their cables. If these tear out, the motor winding or the electronics may also be destroyed.

After you've ensured the perfect state of the mechanics, you should always switch on the radio control transmitter first. In this way, the quadcopter is always receiving a useful signal when you turn it on. You must make sure that the gas sticks are in the idle position. Most systems have a built-in safety feature here, so they first expect an idle gas position after switching on before you can turn the motors on. However, it can't be stated that every system will work this way. Then you switch the quadcopter on. It is possible that it first autonomously performs a calibration of its sensors. In most cases a LED lights up after a few seconds to show that the system is now ready to fly.

3.6   Range test of the radio control

With quadcopters the electrically conductive carbon is often used as a framework. Therefore, the range is usually somewhat restricted compared with model airplanes. For the optimal function, the receiver antenna doesn't like having any other conductive material around.

Therefore, you should perform a range test. Move away from the quadcopter and start the motors with the transmitter. Here, a system configurable by PC shows benefits. With some systems, the quality of the received signal can be tracked and it can then be read via the interface – similar to a flight recorder. Bidirectional radio controls with a 2.4 GHz base often have functions that allow the quality of the received signal to be read directly on the radio control. This is a plus point for this technology.

3.7   Motor check

If everything was done right, the motors can be turned on by a button or stick movement. They run fine in idle when the throttle stick of the radio control is down. Now, the gas functions can be tested. With a higher throttle position all the four motors should turn faster in equal measure. A running-in of the brushless motors is not necessary. With brushed motors, emptying one or two battery charges at half throttle would increase the lifetime. In this way, the brushes get shaped correctly. The throttle stick should not be moved to full throttle first. Now the nick and the roll functions can be tested. Once the stick is pushed in one direction, this motor should rotate more slowly, and in the opposite direction faster. With the yaw functions two opposing motors must always rotate faster or slower.

Once the motors are started, you should in each case once again check the correct control functions on the ground. If you push the nick and roll stick in a certain direction, the corresponding booms should tilt there. If you give more gas, all propellers should rotate faster.

3.8   Spectators while practicing

Throughout the practice phase you must take great care that you can concentrate fully on your aircraft. Particularly as a beginner you should make sure that no spectators are on the airfield. They may mean well and want to provide support, or are perhaps curious and waiting for the exciting model to take off, but they are out of place at this stage. At the end of the day, someone who is practicing is just practicing and is not at an airshow. If there are still people who do not want to miss this supposed spectacle under any circumstances, you should ask them always to stay a safe distance of some meters behind you. They should never get into the field of view, because they might distract you during the flight. In addition, while practicing, the aircraft will mostly be flying in front of you and land immediately if it goes out of sight. It can be dangerous for spectators when a quadcopter is getting out of control. Figure 17 shows how it is meant to be.

Figure 17: There shouldn't be any spectators while you are practicing. If someone really wants to watch, he should always stand behind the pilot.

Of course, a little more experienced quadcopter pilot can allow spectators when he masters some maneuvers. But this is always under consideration of Figure 17. It is in the end the decision of the model pilot when he is ready to show his flying skills to others.

3.9   First takeoff for trimming

Just as a beginner, you can't easily trim the quadcopter while you are flying it. So you should try to trim it with the observation of a first takeoff. First move about five meters from the system and push the gas stick on the transmitter. The quadcopter should at first take off about 50 cm from the ground. Then you take the stick back for landing. All other sticks, i.e. yaw, nick and roll, remain in the neutral position if possible. Now you can observe how the system behaved. As a general rule, for a quadcopter less trim is demanded than for helicopters, because the mechanics are simpler and also symmetrical. If the rotational speeds of the four motors are not very different from each other, and each left and right rotating propellers are mounted correctly, the system takeoff will be more or less straight and it won't rotate either.

It can happen, however, that the system in flight turns something or that it doesn't land at the same place as it was launched. In this case, you should repeat the takeoff again and observe whether it shows the same characteristics again. At this low flight altitude the so-called ground effect occurs. This is air turbulence caused by the rotating propellers themselves. The ground effect can also cause turns and different landing points of the system. But if the second takeoff shows the same characteristics as the first one, you can re-trim a little. For a right turn a little yaw trim should be given to the left and vice versa. In a forward movement you should give some nick trim to the rear, and vice versa, or in a left movement a little roll trim to the right and vice versa. The symmetrical design of the quadcopters has only slight inaccuracies, as discussed above. Therefore, you should always trim just a very little.

4.   First flight

Now you really start your flight experience. Mastering the so-called rear hovering is the most important basis to later perform more complicated flight maneuvers. You should therefore spend sufficient time on this chapter and practice it with many battery charges, until you master this flight position. Figure 18 shows the acquired knowledge at the end.

This is not equally difficult to learn with all quadcopters. In particular, systems with GPS or those with ground sensors can even perform automatic take-off or landing maneuvers. However, the following information is intended for quadcopters that are flown without this technical support. If this sensor support is available, it also makes sense to fly the following maneuvers first with its support.

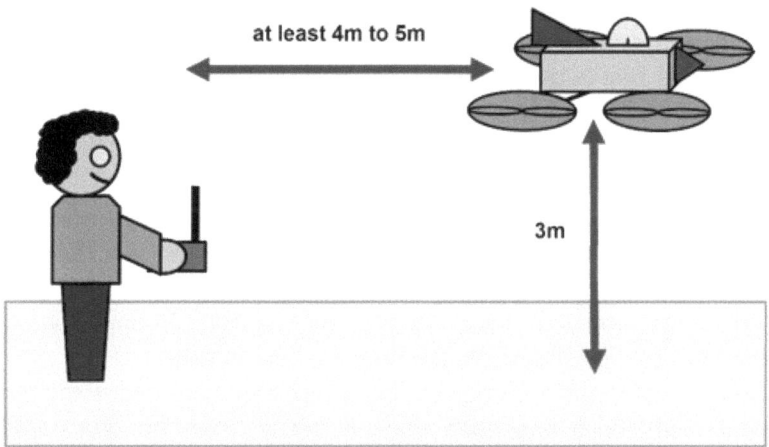

Figure 18: Rear hovering.

The end of the quadcopter should hover at a constant height of about three meters and at a constant distance of about five meters in front of the pilot. It should not turn away in the yaw axis, but always float in the same positon in front of the pilot. Thus he always looks at the rear of the quadcopter. This has the great advantage that during flight, the stick movements of the radio control always correspond to the direction of movement of the quadcopter. The skills that are learned here are on the one hand keeping the height constant using the throttle stick and on the other hand controlling the nick, roll and yaw axis. For this, all physical movements are practiced and also all sticks of the radio control are used. The ground effect was already mentioned above. It involves an unquiet hovering below a height of a little more than the rotor diameter. If you were hovering at this very low height, the system would fly in the turbulences reflected from the ground. It would therefore be very rough and would break away to one side or the other. Of course, this is not suitable for this first exercise. Therefore you need to levitate the quadcopter already in the first phase a bit higher. The quadcopter is at a safe altitude above a height of around half a meter.

4.1　Takeoff

Now we are getting started with the first flight. For this you should try as the first target to keep the system one meter in the air. Here you are trying first of all to balance just with the nick and roll stick of the transmitter. This is in most cases the control stick on the right side. So for the moment you ignore the yaw stick.

For this you place the quadcopter at a distance of five meters, as previously discussed, and you have the rear in view. If a little wind is present, you place the nose – i.e. the front part – into the wind. With more wind you should not start the first flight. In any case, for the take- off you should always have the rear in view.

Now you can start the engines and give a little more gas. If the trim described above has been done correctly, then the quadcopter should no longer rotate around the vertical axis at least before takeoff. If it does still do that at this time, you need to reduce the gas and trim again a little bit. In any case, before each flight you should take care, that you always place the quadcopter with the rear in view.

Now you give a powerful burst of gas, so that the system is soon flying at the desired height of one meter. Then reduce the gas a little, but not too much, so that it can maintain this altitude. Now you concentrate first on the balancing of the nick and roll axes. When the quadcopter tends backwards and moves towards you, you are giving a slight pitching motion forwards. As it moves forwards, away from you, you pull the nick stick slightly towards you. You do exactly the same with the roll axis. So if it drifts to the right, you move the stick of the radio control slightly to the left. If it drifts to the left, you move it to the right. When the quadcopter slightly turns around the vertical axis, you should try to turn yourself in that direction, in order that you again have the view to the rear. Only then will the quadcopter move in the same direction as the stick. If it moves slightly away, you can also move a little behind it to always keep approximately the distance of five meters. Of course, you also need to adjust the height with the gas stick. Push it forwards if it's flying too low and pull it back if it is flying too high. Depending on how large the practice space is, you can do that for quite a long time. With a bit more practice you can then try to keep the quadcopter hovering in the same place. You may need to turn yourself a little with it, because you initially don't control the yaw axis simultaneously with nick and roll. Please land immediately if you no longer have the view to the rear and also when the distance is much more than five meters.

4.2   More flights

As a student pilot you will quickly notice that the first flights are quite nerve-wracking. This can also increase the adrenaline quickly. So flights of half a minute are rather the exception at the beginning. They are more in the range of ten or twenty seconds. Therefore, you will make a lot of such flights. However, you must always pay attention to the charge status of the battery. Today's systems usually have a total flight time of about ten minutes and even longer with one battery charge. You should definitely make sure that there are sufficient reserves in the accumulated time of the flights. In the simplest case, a stopwatch can help here. Many systems also have built-in warning systems. This is either a flight time display on the transmitter or a sound or light signal is emitted when the battery charge is empty. In any case, there should always be sufficient thrust reserve available, because a landing with an almost empty battery is not always easy. Besides, it also increases its lifetime and thus the number of charge cycles if it is not completely empty at the end of the flights.

This is the phase of practice which you really cannot cut out. And correspondingly it also requires your full attention. Bit by bit you will then also have some successful experiences. You will notice that you have ever more capacity free to move not only the nick and roll stick, but in addition also the yaw and throttle stick. Soon you will be able to control the quadcopter also around the yaw axis. Then you also have the view to the quadcopter's rear at all times, and you no longer need to rotate together with the system.

You should get used from the beginning not looking at the stick of the radio control during the flight. The view should always be directed towards the flying quadcopter. It is there where the movements initiated with the remote control take place. And it is these movements which you need to control with the radio control.

4.3   Landing

Each flight is only as good as the subsequent landing. This is true for each hovering, no matter how beautiful and successful it was. Damage almost never occurs in flight, but only when the aircraft is more or less smoothly coming into contact with the ground. Therefore, in the first flights the quadcopter should only be hovering at a height of about one meter. If at this height the pilot has the feeling that he can't master his quadcopter any more, he should quickly pull back the gas control stick. This can be, for example, because the quadcopter breaks out to one side, or because it rotates too quickly around the vertical axis, or because you lost the orientation to the system. Most quadcopters which are suitable for practice survive without damage a hard landing from one meter. In doubt it is always safer to take away the gas. With incorrect control commands things can get even worse. For example, the quadcopter can gain more altitude or will fly further away. If your quadcopter is already floating slightly higher than one meter because of a slightly overly strong gas position and if you are also concerned that you could lose control or the orientation of the quadcopter then you should bring the pitch and roll stick to the middle position.

Try first to withdraw the gas gradually, so that the landing is not quite as rough. But that may be easier said or written in the theory here than done in practice. The best case is of course always the one in which you want to make the landing of your own free will. So this is then a controlled hover. Here you take the gas only slightly back, so that the quadcopter passes into a slow descending flight. You continue controlling the pitch and roll stick and try to keep the position as best as possible. Additionally, depending on the extent of your practice, you can also try to control the yaw axis with the corresponding stick, so that you always have the view to the rear also during the landing phase.

Once the quadcopter is then quite close to making contact with the ground, you take the gas even further back and it sets down on the floor. Now drive the motors into idle and turn them off completely.

With some systems, it can be observed that after a slightly harder landing the quadcopter is revving up the engines and hops again to a height of a few centimeters. Only then does it finally set down on the floor. This happens due to the internal controllers and the sensors, as these also respond to changes in the accelerations.

4.4   Hovering above ground characteristics

To be able to float on the spot as best as possible, there is also another possibility. You can also try to orientate yourself on ground characteristics. There are in the technology and research fields systems which can do this autonomously. These take photographs from the ground using a built-in camera and try autonomously to float above specific characteristics. This can be for example the transition between asphalt and grass or a structure of the garden plates or even large leaves. What is an advantage of technology can also serve as an exercise for quadcopter pilots. You identify the characteristics and have them in an enlarged view, while your concentration is still dedicated to the quadcopter.

This is not suitable for all pilots. Especially at the beginning of the practice phase it means even more attention to something that does not concern the quadcopter itself. However, for a more advanced phase of practicing, it can be quite helpful.

4.4   Rear hovering

Figure 19: Rear hovering, view to the rear side of a quadcopter.

With even more practice you can then try to hover at a distance of five meters and a height of three meters. Of course, you should then use all functions of both sticks of the radio control. In summary, these are:

- the nick and roll function to keep the position
- the gas function to keep the height
- the yaw function to keep the orientation and the view to the rear of the quadcopter

The flight times should now be even longer. Gradually you will now reach flight times of more than half a minute, without much sweat of brow. You no longer need breaks between the flights. At the end you should be so far advanced that you do not notice how time passes – that time literally just flew by. At the beginning of the practice phase you will sometimes feel flight stress rather than flight fun, but the flight fun will increase with the mastery of the rear hovering.

Now you're a so-called rear hoverer. The definition of this could be described as follows: you have mastered the flight as shown in Figure 18 and you are able to fly for several minutes up to an entire battery charge and without sweat.

However, the most important characteristic of a rear hoverer should be achieved by the end of this chapter: you feel a satisfaction during the flight and the flight fun begins.

5.   Rotating away and first flight figures

Many quadcopter pilots are keenly interested in technology. For example, they want to take photos or films with onboard cameras. Systems with GPS and electronic compass sometimes have an operating mode installed with which you can control the system so that it always moves in the same direction as the stick, regardless of its orientation. For this reason, many pilots have no interest in complex flight figures and always operate their quadcopter in the rear hovering. That's one more reason why you must master rear hovering.

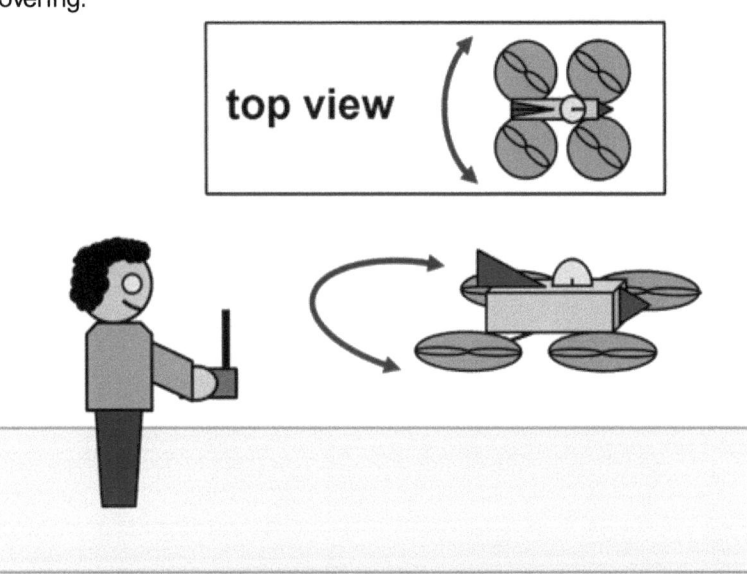

Figure 20: rotating away from the rear hover, yaw

However, if you also master rotating the system away from the rear hovering, using the yaw stick, then it is also possible to fly figures in the air. Figure 20 shows what is meant by this.

Here now arises a problem that the movements of the radio control stick for nick and roll no longer point accurately in the same direction as the quadcopter. One should imagine the extreme case where this would be so far rotated away that the nose is pointing towards you. Therefore you would see it from the front. In this flight attitude, these functions would then be completely mirrored. It is of course clear that this would require more concentration and practice. And exactly this will be described and learned in this and the next sections.

5.1 Sligtly rotating, rear circle

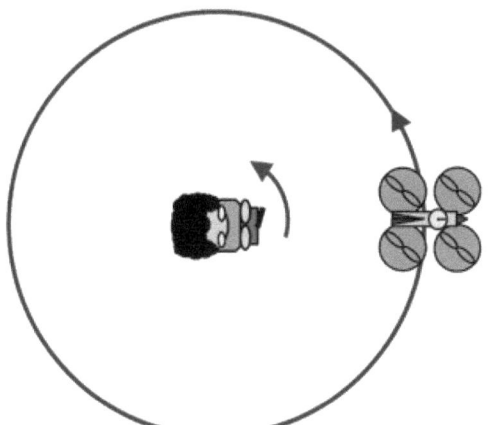

Figure 21: Rear circle.

For all that follows, it is essential that you master rear hovering safely. Just as you performed there a landing in the case of emergency, you will be trying here again and again to turn back to the rear hovering position. Of course you should not fly too high again, so you can reduce the gas to land if you lose orientation. That would, however, be a good indication that you should read the chapter on the rear hovering position again and practice it again in detail.

As a first exercise you should carefully rotate the quadcopter away in one direction, in the vertical axis. Here you can also turn yourself with one or two steps, so that you again have the view to the rear of the quadcopter. So you again find yourself in the rear hover position, only you slightly rotated along with your quadcopter, compared to the start.

If you consistently do this over and over again, then in the end you will have rotated 360 degrees around your own axis. Then you have positioned the quadcopter repeatedly in the rear hovering position. And for the first time, you have already drawn a simple figure in the sky, namely the so-called rear circle. Figure 21 shows this.

But you should not aim for perfection in this procedure straight away – you can only perform it slowly, so that you do not get dizzy. Of course, this is not a nice round circle at the beginning. But after a few rounds you can keep a more or less constant distance to the quadcopter. So it is getting closer to the circular shape.

5.2   Side hovering

Bit by bit you should try to turn yourself less and less. Then the quadcopter will be slightly sideways to your position. You'll become more confident with these movements. Eventually you will be able to remain on one spot, without turning yourself.

In this way you can easily rotate the quadcopter to one side and the other. The rotation around the vertical axis is called yaw in technical jargon, named after the stick on the radio control.

At first you'll master the rotation only at a very small angle. Then you can steadily enlarge it. And after a while you'll be able to control your quadcopter as shown in Figure 22.

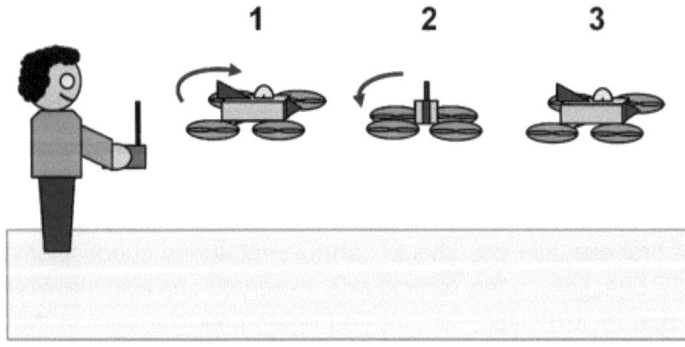

Figure 22: From rear hovering to side hovering and back again.

You can rotate away from the rear hovering position (phase 1) a quarter turn into the side hovering position (phase 2). Here the quadcopter hovers for a short time at a right angle in front of you. Then you turn it back to its original position (phase 3). Even this relatively simple move will not work smoothly at the beginning. But after several attempts it will get better and better. Eventually you'll be able to fly the figure quite well.

At the beginning there is still a big difference between whether you immediately rotate back to the rear hovering position (phase 3) after reaching the side hovering position (phase 2), or whether you can hold this position for a certain length of time. The latter requires some more practice. Even the author, who has mastered all of the flight attitudes presented here, must practice this until he can do it again after a long flight break of several weeks.

Thus, the technique shown in Figure 22 can be said to have been mastered when you can rotate from phase 1 to phase 2 in a controlled manner, and then remain in that position for a certain length of time and then rotate to phase 3, so back to the rear hovering position.

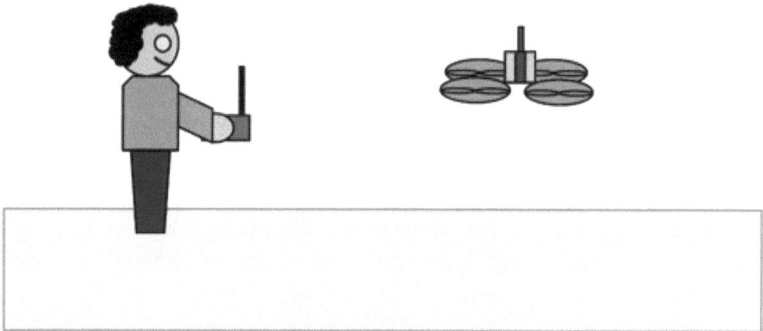

Figure 23: Side hovering.

The rotation to the other side must also be practiced well. Once you have mastered the technique shown in Figure 22, it will be relatively easy for you to also rotate to the other side, again up to a quarter of a full turn. In the end you master this figure with the rotation to both sides equally well and you can in particular also remain in phase 2, so in the side hovering position. So you can rotate the quadcopter to both sides in the side hovering position and control it so that it remains on the spot. Figures 23 and 24 show the side hovering position.

Figure 24: Side hovering of a quadcopter in '+'-configuration, view from the pilot.

5.3   Side eight

Now it's time to fly your first self-contained figure. That's a side eight. Figure 31 shows with a view from above what is meant by that. The advantage of a side eight is that you can fly both curves with the rear hovering technique, in addition with a nick movement forwards. That is, in the illustration, where the two arrows are drawn. In between, the quadcopter must be controlled with side hovering, as was practiced in the last figures. In particular, throughout the figure you never have to fly the difficult flight attitude 'nose flight'. This attitude has not yet been discussed, but the quadcopter would then fly towards you and the stick movements for nick and roll would be reversed.

The forward flight is always realized with an additional slight movement about the nick axis. Also the speed is controlled in this way. A higher speed is realized with a little more nick and a lower speed with a little less nick. The side eight flight figure is then relatively easy to learn if you mastered the preceding exercises well.

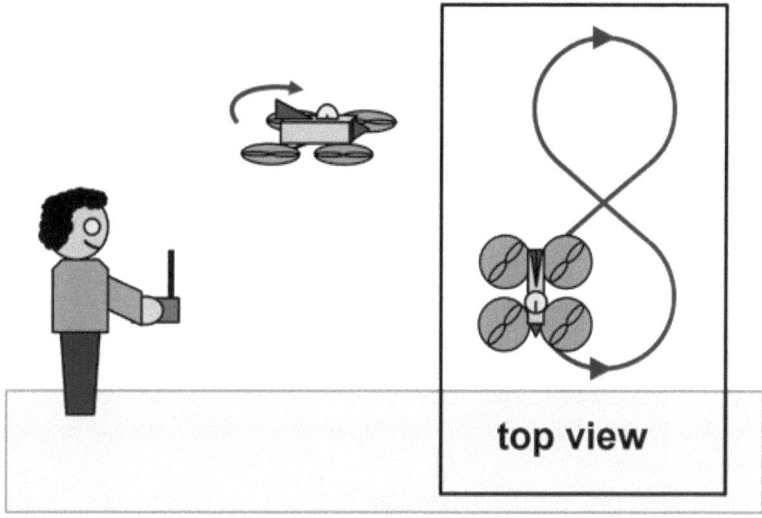

Figure 25: Side eight.

The first side eight will probably still be fairly angular – there will be rotations on the spot and then followed by straight forward movements. But once you have managed a whole eight, you will find great pleasure in it. Gradually, you'll learn to fly it so that it is as beautiful as drawing with a pencil directly in the air. The size of the figure is somewhat dependent on the visibility and the size of the quadcopter, and also on the available space. At the initial stage you should not fly overly large side eights.

With a little more practice you can then fly it at different heights and in different sizes. Then you will not only see the orientation of the quadcopter, but you also feel it because of the flight behavior. Then you will fly even larger side eights.

5.4   Loss of orientation

Here follows a small discussion on the loss of orientation. Once you learn to fly your first flight figures, you'll rotate your quadcopter around the yaw axis, as described above. The one time or another in the exercise phase, it will happen that the orientation gets lost in the air.

This is a difficult situation because you no longer know in which direction a nicking or rolling motion is working. Here you should just release the nick and roll stick and try to take away some gas, so that you can land reasonably safely. Once you lose the orientation in the air, in practice it's almost impossible for the beginner to win it back again.

5.5   Rectangle

With all maneuvers which have been discussed so far, it could be avoided that the quadcopter flies against the pilot. That will change in this section.

Figure 26 shows a flight in a rectangle.

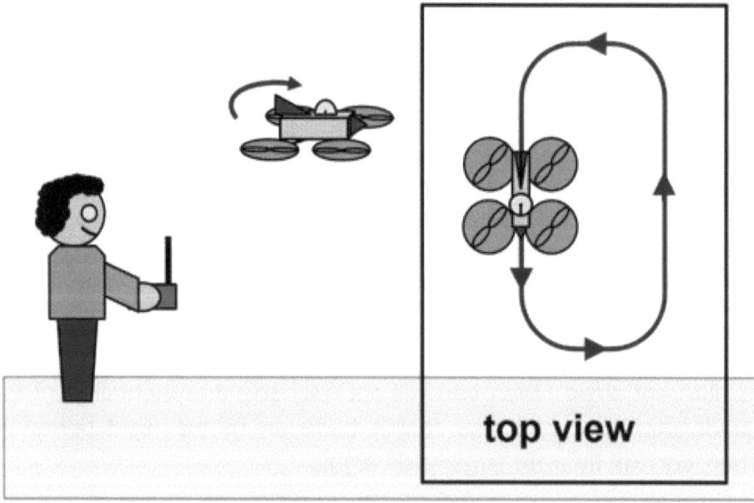

Figure 26: Rectangle.

This figure is comparable only at first sight with the side eight discussed above. On closer inspection, one realizes that it contains a new flight phase.

Here the quadcopter is flying against the pilot and therefore also all movements of the nick and roll stick are performed reversed at the quadcopter, as seen from the pilot's perspective.

This figure is therefore more difficult to fly than the side eight. At the very beginning you will realize that you stay as short a time as possible in this phase of flight. So you will perform about a 180° rotation from one side hover (in the figure from bottom to top) to the other side hover (in the figure from top to bottom).

Thus, at first this will not be a rectangle, but something like a triangle. First, you will fly in this way a complete figure. Then you will gradually try to lengthen the flight phase with against flight, so a true rectangle is actually created. Also this you will master in the end at different heights and in different sizes.

5.6 Side circle

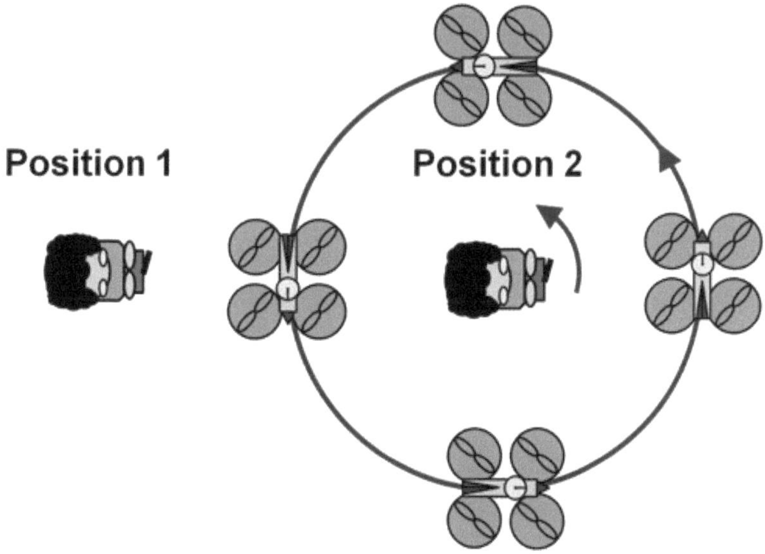

Figure 27: Side circle with two positions of the pilot.

The side circle is a very similar maneuver to the rectangle. It is shown in Figure 27. In contrast to the rectangle this is not only a combination of single straight flight passages and rotations in one place, but here you also try a continuous coupling of the rotation and the straight flying during the entire flight. You'll try in practice to start with the rectangle. Then you make the 90° rotation a little rounder, by giving slight nick in addition to yaw. This you can then develop further until the next 90° rotation fits seamlessly to the previous one. Thus, the phases in which you flew straight forward gradually disappear entirely.

So you fly the side circle, at first again not quite round, but later ever closer to the figure. Now it is also time to think about your own position in the flight figures. The position in which you find yourself when passing from the rectangle to the side circle flight figure is position 1. Here you do not move yourself and you always have the quadcopter in view in front of you.

Maybe you master the flight figure even better in position 2. In this you find yourself right in the center of the figure, but during the flight you need to rotate around your own axis, so that you always see the quadcopter. The term side circle can be explained quite well with position 2. Throughout the maneuver, the pilot always sees his quadcopter from the side. The side circle can thus also be compared with the rear circle of Figure 21. There one always has the view to the rear.

5.7   Lengthwise eight

A distinction is made between the side eight and the lengthwise eight discussed above, because the lengthwise eight is more difficult to control. Figure 28 shows this flight figure.

The pilot is not flying this figure at the side, but lengthwise to himself. In particular, there is in comparison to the side eight a long flight phase during which the quadcopter flies against him. The previous maneuvers already contained elements of against flight. Therefore even this eight will be safely controllable after a little practice.

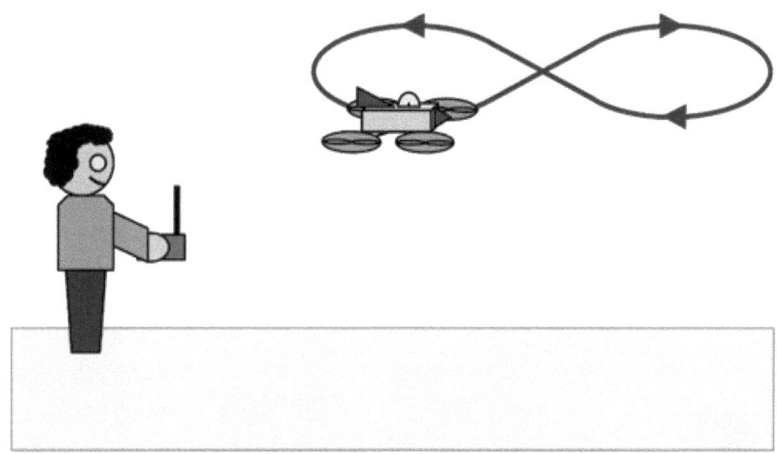

Figure 28: Lengthwise eight.

Again, it is very important that you have enough space in front of you. With against flight it is also very important that you can rotate the quadcopter away in time before it flies too close to you. In an open field, it is also possible that you move to the rear when the space in front is no longer sufficient. In an emergency, a landing with idle gas position can also help here.

6. More challenging flight maneuvers

6.1 Nose hovering

With all maneuvers presented up to this point, against flight has always been coupled with a forward motion. It will be a little more difficult when the quadcopter should hover this on the spot. Figures 29 to 31 show what is meant here.

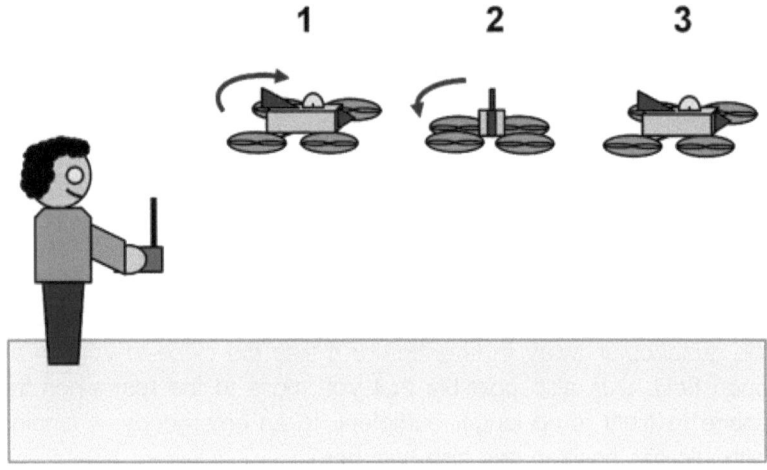

Figure 29: From rear hovering to side hovering to nose hovering.

This hovering position is called nose hovering. You can achieve this as shown in Figure 29 if you start from the rear hovering position (1) and rotate first away to side hovering (2) and then try to continue rotating. The front part of helicopters and quadcopters is called the nose. If you can see this nose from the front during the flight, so if you have the view to the front of the quadcopter, this is called nose hovering (3) or nose flight.

In this flight attitude, the movements of the nick and roll axes are exactly opposite to the movements of the sticks of the radio control. So if you pull the nick stick, the quadcopter tilts backwards and starts to fly away from you. If you push the nick stick, it tilts forwards and the aircraft begins flying towards you.

Analogously, a movement of the roll stick to the left causes a tilt to the right and a move to the right causes a tilt to the left, as seen from the pilot's position. The quadcopter starts to drift in the corresponding inclinations. Therefore it also moves in the opposite direction to the sticks, seen from the pilot's position.

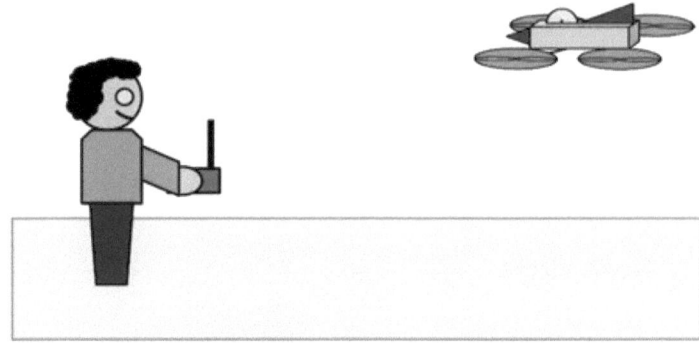

Figure 30: Nose hovering or nose flight.

Figure 31: Nose hovering with an octocopter.

45

To safely control this flight attitude, it again requires some additional practice. The goal is, however, that in the end the quadcopter is hovering without any drift motion in one direction or another. The nose should always be visible from the front and it should hover exactly in one place, as it is shown in Figure 29. Once you safely master flying in the rear, the side and the nose hovering positions and the quadcopter remains in these positions for as long as you want it to, you can build upon many other flight maneuvers.

If you master rear, side and nose hovering, these can be combined with the forward flight or lateral drift movements. Here you find more maneuvers which are good to learn.

6.2   Nose circle

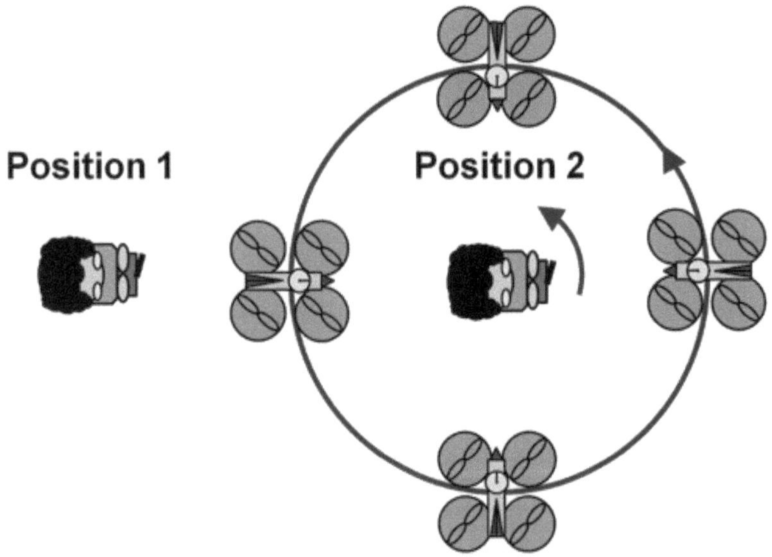

Figure 32: Nose circle with two positions of the pilot.

Figure 32 shows the nose circle. It can be compared with the side circle in Figure 27. As with the side circle, you can also fly the nose circle in two different positions from the pilot. Again position 2 is a little easier to control. Here the pilot is in the center of the circle and he rotates again along with the quadcopter.

At first, you bring it into a stable nose hovering position. Then you begin to drift it using the roll stick of the radio control. In the nose hovering position, the quadcopter again moves in the opposite direction, seen from the pilot's position. At the same time you must also balance the orientation with the yaw stick and you also need to rotate yourself. With a little practice a smooth circular motion is soon achieved. Then, the quadcopter is always hovering at the same distance from the pilot and he always has the view to the nose. Another challenge is also that the inclination of the roll axis always remains the same throughout the whole circle. Then the quadcopter always drifts at the same speed.

Then you can also try to stand in position 1 and fly a nose circle with your aircraft in front of you. This way the maneuver is slightly more difficult to master. From the view of the pilot, you must change the hovering positions of the quadcopter several times. The sequence during a circle is: nose hovering – side hovering – rear hovering – side hovering again – nose hovering. You must also always move the roll stick and simultaneously ensure that the circle emerges reasonably nicely.

Figure 33: Nose circle, view from the pilot ('+'-configuration).

47

6.3   Rear circle

The pilot's position 2 of the rear circle shown in Figure 34 has already been discussed; see Figure 21.

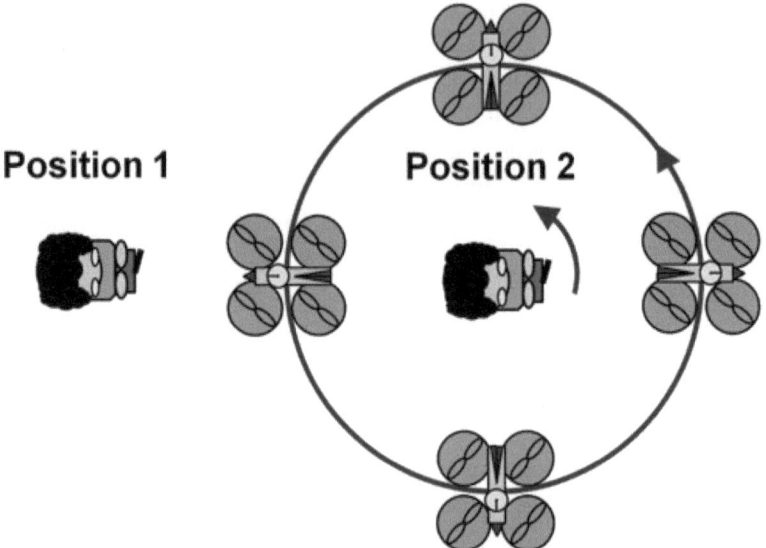

Figure 34: Rear circle with two pilot positions.

In this position, after all, only the rear of the quadcopter is in view. Therefore, it is also a very simple maneuver and it is suitable for beginners. From position 1, the rear circle is much more difficult to master. It is similarly difficult as the above-discussed nose circle from the same position 1.

Because the pilot is not rotating along with the quadcopter, here again the hovering positions are changed successively, so rear, side and nose hovering. It makes sense to start the figure at some distance with a view to the rear. Then you rotate the quadcopter left into side hovering. In the nose hovering it is located closest to yourself and after you have rotated it to the right again into the side hovering, you turn it back to the rear hovering at the end.

Again, you will not succeed immediately in obtaining a beautiful round trajectory, which you can fly with a smooth movement of the roll stick and a constant speed. But once you have flown some circles, each one is better than the last.

6.4   Promenade

The term promenade comes from the French and means to walk. Figure 35 shows how this is to be understood. The quadcopter remains in one place. But the pilot moves or walks around it. Also for this flight figure you must master all hovering positions. Starting with the rear hovering position, you see your aircraft after a quarter turn in the side hovering, and after a half turn in the nose hovering. In the second half of the figure you see it in the side hovering and at the end in the rear hovering again.

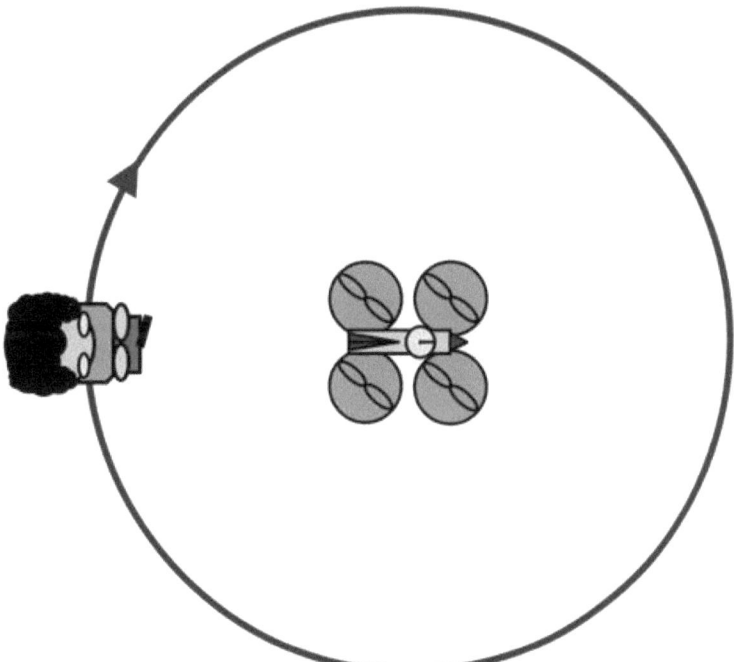

Figure 35: Promenade, a walk of the pilot.

The difficulty with this figure is that the quadcopter must be hovering in one place at all times. In other words, this also means that the quality of the promenade flight maneuver is measured by how successful this attempt is.

Therefore you must walk and at the same time you have to stay calm, in order that the quadcopter does not suddenly drift away. At the beginning you will be happy if you can just keep at least the orientation of the quadcopter at all times. As with the previous flight movements, again some practice is necessary until this works very well.

6.5   Pirouette and circle Pirouette

A pirouette is a rotation of 360 degrees around the yaw axis, as shown in Figure 36. This maneuver is in itself relatively simple to master. It is important that you can perform the rotation on the spot.

Figure 36: Pirouette, rotation of 360° around the yaw axis.

Then you can combine several pirouettes with other maneuvers. To perform the pirouette, you leave the nick and roll stick in the middle position and you move only the yaw stick in one direction or the other.

50

With this and the following maneuvers, it can happen with some quadcopters that the built-in sensors will lose some orientation after such a rotation. Not every quadcopter is adapted and designed for such complicated flight maneuvers. This is similar to humans, who can also become dizzy with twists around their own axis. So the quadcopter may rotate a little further, even though you put the yaw stick of the radio control in the neutral position again. This can especially be a problem if you make more than one revolution. If it is not stabilized and the rotation does not stop after some hovering, you should immediately land.

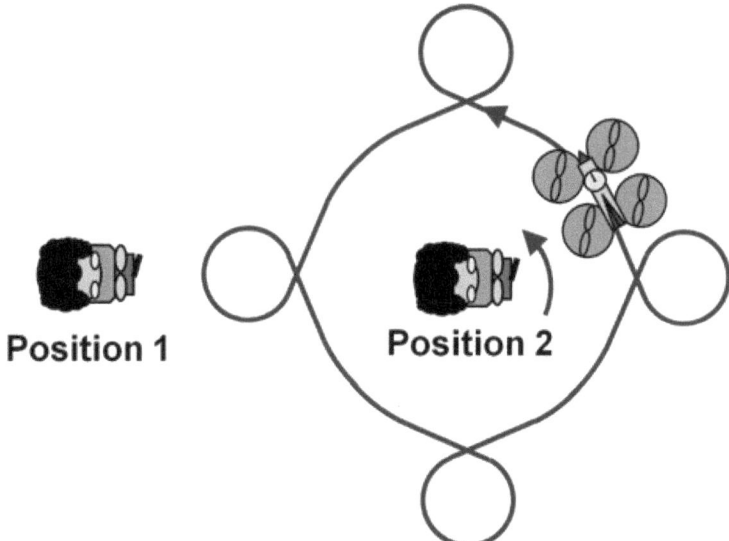

Figure 37: Circle pirouette.

Now it is also possible to form a circular flight with a combination of several such pirouettes. The resulting flight figure is shown in Figure 37 and is called a circle pirouette. Here a circle pirouette with four pirouettes is shown. Of course, circle pirouettes with fewer or even more pirouettes are also possible.

You can fly the circle pirouette in pilot position 1 or 2. The level of difficulty is similar.

6.6   Funnel, Pie Dish

This flight figure is also called 'pie dish' in some literature. To fly, you start with a nose circle as shown in Figure 32. You fly it with a relatively small radius in pilot position 1, so that you are performing the whole maneuver in front of you, and you are standing on one spot. While you fly several rotations with nose circles, you change the nick angle slightly from the horizontal direction to the center of the circle. And you also give a little more gas to keep the height. Actually the quadcopter would begin to drift forwards. Since it is in a permanent rotation because of the nose circle, with a little practice the center of the funnel remains still in one place.

Depending on your progress you can then enlarge the pitch angle more and more. Pilots of model helicopters speak of an actual funnel from an inclination of the pitch axis of 45°, but even smaller angles of around 20° to 30° promise already quite 'funnely' flight experiences.

Especially also in this maneuver, it is possible with some quadcopters that the sensors lose their orientation during flight. Then you need to land after the funnel. Not all manufacturers have developed their quadcopters for such aerobatic flying figures. When buying, you do not yet notice whether it is made for such maneuvers or not. The quality of the sensors, also known as the Inertial Measurement Unit (IMU), determines together with the axis controllers for nick, roll and yaw whether funnels, pirouettes or the maneuvers described in the next section can be performed well. Many camera-carrying systems are less suitable for flying such figures.

In Figure 38, the funnel is shown as described above, thus with the nose towards the center. In principle it is also possible to carry out the funnel with the rear towards the center, so based on a rear circle. The difficulty of such a funnel is even slightly greater.

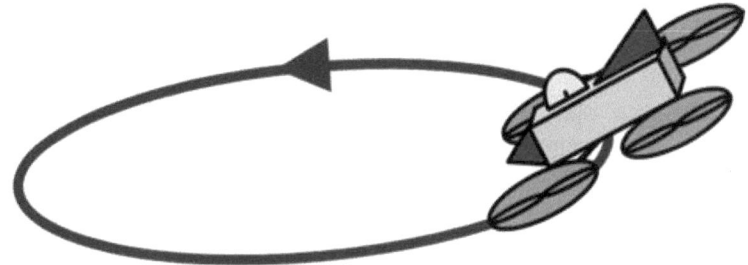

Figure 38: Funnel.

6.7   Tic- Toc and snake

The discussed flight maneuvers are all oriented on the RC helicopter models. But a quadcopter can't fly stably overhead, so in the supine position. For this purpose, the rotors should not be controlled by speed but by pitch. But it is precisely the speed control which results in the very simple mechanics of the quadcopter, and therefore there are (almost) no pitch controlled rotor systems. For this reason, with the pitch-controlled RC helicopters more difficult flight maneuvers are possible. Of all of these, only the two in the title will be discussed here – tick-tock and snake. But these are simplified, so that the flight with quadcopters is also quite possible.

Figure 39: Tic-toc.

You can fly the tick-tock maneuver in its simplest form, as illustrated in Figure 39. Here, the rear and the nose move alternatively up and down by using the nick stick. So two end positions are obtained, like the pendulum of an old clock. The name has its origin in the tick-tock noise of a clock. With a quadcopter you can also do a tick-tock around the roll axis. You need to move the roll stick back and forth and the quadcopter moves to the left and right.

With aerobatic helicopter models one can also fly the tick-tock maneuver in completely different attitudes, for example with a half rotation around the longitudinal axis. However, it is common in all of the figures that the model always moves back and forth in two positions. The snake figure must also be flown in a somewhat simplified manner for speed-controlled quadcopters. With the tail or nose ahead, you string together several equal circle segments. This results in a serpentine-shaped flight movement. Then you repeat this flight in the opposite direction. At the end, the quadcopter is back in the same position as at the beginning of the figure. With pitch-controlled RC helicopters, additional roll movements can be performed. Then they move from normal to inverted flight and back again.

7.   Speed flight and loops, flips

In speed flight the quadcopter is inclined forwards in the nick direction. The more strongly it is inclined, the greater is the proportion of propeller thrust force which is acting in a forwards direction and the faster is the forward flight. In order to keep the height you will also need more thrust, because the proportion of upwardly acting thrust force is smaller. You reach the maximum speed when the gas stick is pushed right to the top. The quadcopter is then inclined as strongly as it is flying horizontally in forward flight. In this way you can do speed flight at 50 km/h or even more.

Quadcopters are admittedly not quite as fast as model airplanes. But they are controlled similarly to them. The roll axis of the quadcopter corresponds to the aileron axis of the model aircraft. It is there often passively stabilized by the V-shape of the wings. For aerobatic models, the V-shape is not very pronounced or even non-existent. Then, the stabilization is done by the ailerons. Such a model airplane is most comparable to the quadcopter in respect of the control.

In contrast to model aircraft, quadcopters are completely symmetrical aircraft. This also means that it doesn't matter whether you incline them forwards or backwards or even in the direction of the roll axis. Their behavior in all directions is always the same. Thus it is possible in principle to fly backwards or sideways with the same maximum speed as forwards. A quadcopter is even more flexible in flight than a model airplane is. This can indeed only fly forwards for aerodynamic reasons.

As with all the flight maneuvers presented above, it is also important with speed flight that you know at all times the current flight position and orientation. Only in this way can you perform the correct control commands. Since in speed flight the quadcopter can fly away quickly, highly visible fuselages help prevent you losing your orientation.

7.1   Height versus speed

It is always possible to generate height from velocity and vice versa. This follows from physics and the principle of energy conservation. A quadcopter located at a certain height has energy stored, namely so-called potential energy. The same goes for a moving quadcopter, so a quadcopter in speed flight has motion energy stored. The law of conservation of energy states that one form of energy can be converted to another. Transferred into practice that means precisely that velocity may arise from height and vice versa. Figures 40 and 41 show what is meant.

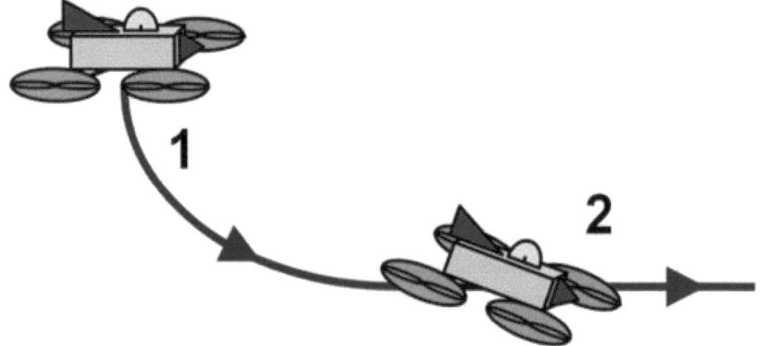

Figure 40: Generating speed from height.

In Figure 40, the quadcopter is first at a certain height in the hover flight. Now it will be slightly inclined with a nick motion. It then immediately loses height and begins to drift. Already some speed arises from the height. If you give a little more nick and thereby also increase the throttle position, the quadcopter again loses some height and will move forwards even faster due to the strong inclination.

The potential energy stored at the beginning is thus helping, so that only a short time later the quadcopter already moves forwards with considerable speed. So if you want to speed up the quadcopter as fast as possible to a final speed, then you will do better if you start from a good height. Even experienced pilots of model airplanes make use of this physical effect in order to reach high speeds. They give full throttle from a certain height while pushing the elevator stick and so they reach a good speed while monitoring the distance to the ground.

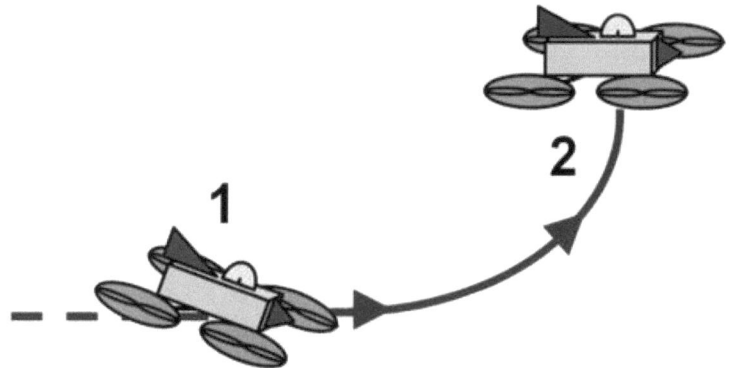

Figure 41: Generating height from speed.

Figure 41 shows the reverse case. Here, height is obtained from a forward movement. At first, the quadcopter is inclined and on a forward flight. It is suddenly brought into the horizontal position, with some nick backwards and pulling of the stick. It slows down here and then immediately gains a bit of height. You can of course also slow down without any gain in height. Then you just need to reduce some gas at the same time.

7.2   Loops and flips
Many quadcopters are steered with an angular control. This means that a movement of the nick or roll stick at the radio control generates a nick or roll axis inclined by a certain angle. The larger the movement of the stick, the greater the angle of the inclination. To perform loops or flips, the quadcopter must fly upside down for a short time. Thus, it must be possible that the angle is momentarily larger than the radio control stick allows.
Some systems therefore have a special feature on the radio control. A hardcoded loop or flip can thus be started and the

quadcopter does it on its own. Especially with many RTF quadcopters, it is nowadays almost standard.

However, if the loop is to be done manually controlled, you have to be able to turn off the angle control at least briefly. For this purpose, in some systems you can change to an angular rate mode. Thus, not the angle itself but its rate of change is controlled. This is done either by a switch on the radio control or the control electronics detects itself that the stick was pulled strongly to the maximum and switches off the angle control for the duration of the loop. But most RTF quadcopters don't include this feature.

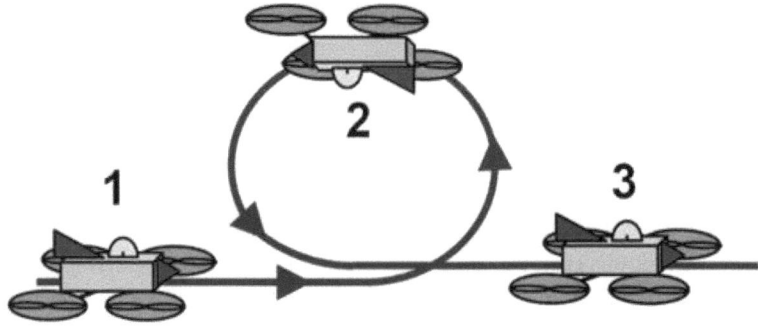

Figure 42: Loop.

Figure 42 shows the flight of a loop. It is very important that you start it from a sufficient height. You should already have some air beneath the propellers. You pull the nick stick strongly and take some gas away. If there is enough space, you can also push the nick stick shortly before, to achieve a little more speed. Ideally, the gas should be very low during the rollover. At this time the thrust is reversed and pointing towards the ground. During the rollover or even shortly after you increase the gas again. The nick stick is then returned to the center position. The quadcopter will return to the hovering position. Beautiful loops are round, as they are shown in the figure. At the beginning, however, you'll be happy if the rollover succeeds without crashing. The loops will gradually get rounder.

The flip is actually something like a loop in a minimum of space.

With a little practice you are also able to do the rollover almost on the spot. A distinction is made between a forward and side flip. The forward flip is a rotation around the nick axis, such as the loop described above. A skilled pilot can perform a forward flip even in the living room within one meter of height. Automated systems also manage it in this narrow space when the pilot pushes the button of the radio control.

The side flip is a rotation around the roll axis. It is also possible to combine such a side flip with forward flight. This results in a roll. But the roll can't be flown quite as nicely as with pitch-controlled helicopters. However, the hovering in the horizontal plane is stable with quadcopters.

Loops and flips can also be combined with additional pirouettes. In this case, you move the yaw stick for the pirouette in addition to the gas, nick and roll sticks for looping, forwards or side flip. Then all sticks are in action. Thus, during the loops and flips one or even several turns around the yaw axis is also performed. The maneuver is then called pirouettes flip, or piroflip in short.

This is again a further increase in the degree of difficulty. Fully savvy pilots even fly multiple such piroflips one after the other. Of course, as with all flight figures, you must make sure that you do not lose the orientation of the quadcopter during the flight. In addition, as with the maneuvers discussed above, the danger is very great that the sensor loses orientation. An immediate landing is then necessary.

You should however only try out the last maneuvers if you have really mastered all the previous ones very well. In the practice phase there will certainly be one or the other broken propeller or boom. Motors can also be damaged. The flight maneuvers which were illustrated and discussed above have increasing levels of difficulty. The more difficult the figures are, the more vulnerable the quadcopter is to crashes and related damage. So if you want to practice maneuvers with quadcopters, you should have a stock of spare parts, if possible.

8.   Literature

[1] Integrierte Navigationssysteme. Sensordatenfusion, GPS und Inertiale Navigation, Jan Wendel, Verlag Oldenbourg 2007, ISBN: 978-3-486-58160-7

[2] Global Positioning Systems, Inertial Navigation, and Integration, Mohinder S. Grewal, Lawrence R. Weill, Angus P. Andrews, Verlag: John Wiley & Sons, Inc. 2007, ISBN: 978-0-470-04190-1

[3] Buchi, Roland, et al. "A remote controlled mobile mini robot." *MHS'96 Proceedings of the Seventh International Symposium on Micro Machine and Human Science*. IEEE, 1996.

[4] Moderne Fernsteuerungen für RC-Flugmodelle, Manfred-Dieter Kotting, Verlag für Technik und Handwerk GmbH, ISBN: 978-3-88180-780-7

[5] Büchi, Roland. "Brushless- Motoren und- Regler." 1. Auflage, Baden-Baden: Verlag für Technik und Handwerk neue Medien GmbH (2013).

[6] Leishman, J.G. (2000). "Principles of Helicopter Aerodynamics". New York, NY: Cambridge University Press. ISBN: 978-0-52185-860-1

[7] Hoffmann, G.M.; Rajnarayan, D.G.; Waslander, S.L.; Dostal, D.; Jang, J.S.; Tomlin, C.J. (November 2004). "The Stanford Testbed of Autonomous Rotorcraft for Multi Agent Control (STARMAC)". In the Proceedings of the 23rd Digital Avionics System Conference. Salt Lake City, UT. pp. 12.E.4/1–10.

[8] Büchi, Roland. *Radio control with 2.4 GHz*. BoD–Books on Demand, 2014., ISBN 978-3732293407